FOREST BOOKS

WASTELANDS OF FIRE

KU SANG was born in Seoul in 1919 but grew up in what is now North Korea. After studying in Japan, he returned and began to work as a journalist. He was forced to flee to the southern part of Korea before the Korean War and for many years was an editorialist and columnist in one of the major Korean newspapers. He has published many volumes of poems and of essays, as well as writing a number of plays, and teaching in universities. Early volumes of poetry include one published in North Korea in 1946, 'Ku Sang' (1951), 'Wastelands of Fire' (1956) and 'Diary of the Fields' (1967). Since 1980 Ku Sang has revised earlier work and published 'The True Appearance of the Word' (1980), 'The Crow' (1981), 'As He Walked Alone' (1981), and 'Even the Knots on Quince Trees' (1984). The present volume of poems selected by the author was published in 1984, under the title 'From Dreyfus' Bench'. In 1986, two 60-poem cycles were published, 'St Christopher's River' and 'Diary of the Fields'. Ku Sang has been chairman of the Korean PEN Section and has been actively involved in Korean literary life. He lives with his wife in Seoul.

ANTHONY TEAGUE was born in Truro (Cornwall) in 1942, and studied Medieval and Modern Languages at Oxford 1960–69. Since 1969, he has been a member of the Community of Taizé (France). He went to Korea in 1980, and studied Korean at Yonsei University (Seoul). He is at present Associate Professor in the English Department of Sogang University (Seoul), where he teaches Medieval and Renaissance literature.

WASTELANDS
OF
FIRE

Selected Poems

of

Ku
Sang

Translated from the Korean
by
Anthony Teague

FOREST BOOKS
LONDON ☆ 1989 ☆ BOSTON

PUBLISHED BY
FOREST BOOKS

20 Forest View, Chingford, London E4 7AY, U.K.
P.O. Box 438, Wayland, MA 01778, U.S.A.

First published 1990

Typeset in Great Britain by Cover to Cover, Cambridge
Printed in Great Britain by BPCC Wheatons Ltd, Exeter

British Library Cataloguing in Publication Data
Sang, Ku
Wastelands of fire: the poetry of Ku Sang.
1. Poetry in Korean, 1945— English texts
I. Title
895.7'14
ISBN 0–948259–82–5

Library of Congress Catalogue Card No

89–85180

FOREST BOOKS gratefully acknowledges the support of the
Korean Culture and Arts Foundation.

Contents

Ku Sang

Introduction

Ku Sang was born in Seoul on 16 September 1919 in a Korea which had been annexed by Japan ten years before and was just beginning to express its deep desire for independence. From his earliest years, he was caught up in the dramatic events, and in the suffering, that are the stuff of modern Korean history. His life has mostly been spent in journalism and the world of public opinion, with periods in political prisons, and in university classrooms. Ku Sang has been a journalist, chief editorialist, foreign correspondent, an essayist, a dramatist, a teacher, and, above all, a poet. He has occupied such positions as the presidency of the Catholic Writers' Association, and of the Korean PEN Section, and he has received many of the highest awards for his work. Ku Sang is one of the most esteemed writers now alive in Korea, and he continues to find many readers.

In 1984, Ku Sang published a set of poems about his early years, 'Even the Knots on Quince Trees', and these poems describe his development through childhood and youth. In the first of them he recalls how, in the early 1920s, his family left Seoul and set off towards the Northern town of Wonsan which he still considers his true home. It will surprise no one familiar with Korean sensibility that the first remembered emotional experience was one of tears.

Ku Sang was born into a Catholic family and his elder brother is among the priests who disappeared into silence and presumed martyrdom in North Korea forty years ago. Ku Sang thought for a time to follow his brother, at least he attended minor seminary for a while, before 'running away'. Later he became a student at the University of Japan in Tokyo, exposed to all the radical currents of Western, particularly French, thought.

Through this time of crisis, in which he studied the philosophy of religions, it was in the end poetry which offered a way forward. Ku Sang returned from his studies a 'follower of isms' and in 1942 became a journalist in what is now North Korea. A few years later he found himself obliged to flee to the South, leaving members of his family in the North, including his mother.

Life in the South was not much more tender, and soon after the end of the Korean War (1950–53) he found himself in prison, having published his 'Democratic Accusations', essays against the corruptions of power. Ku Sang often mentions the cavities in his lungs, the result of the tuberculosis contracted in the course of these experiences.

In 1946, before escaping to the South, he published a first collection of poems in Wonsan. The experience of the Korean War is recorded in the 'Wasteland Poems', first published in 1956. Here we find clearly the sense of national unity, the refusal to accept the division of Korea, which mark many of Ku Sang's poems. An important feature in these war poems is the rejection of all artifice. The poet offers simple evocations of scenes, or of nature, without complex poetic effects, and without too much explicit moralizing.

The theme of the world's impermanence has also become one of Ku Sang's main themes, in part by way of a pun. The 'Sang' of his name is the Chinese character meaning 'enduring', 'permanent', and in philosophical contexts it is part of the quest for the unchanging Real that is expressed, for example, in the opening lines of Lao Tzu. One group of Ku Sang's poems, particularly personal ('Impermanent I'), is entitled in Korean 'Ku-Sang-Mu-Sang', 'Mu' corresponding to the 'im' of 'impermanence'.

Ku Sang's poetry is frequently made rich in sense and allusion through his use of Chinese characters full of abstract, philosophical meanings that are often difficult, even for the present generation of young Koreans, and which cannot be represented by any equivalent in English translation. Yet the starting point is usually some very simple experience of nature, or of daily life. Time after time, the theme of the river returns, as the best focus for thoughts about continuity and renewal, sin and redemption, past and future, time and eternity . . .

The influence of Buddhism is strong in many of Ku Sang's poems, such as we find, for example, in the recently expanded (1986) 'St Christopher's River'. He is fascinated, like so many, by the ambivalence of the link between man and the material universe, by the challenge that physical existence, caught between time and eternity, represents. Indeed, one of the English words he feels particularly attracted by is the word 'metaphysical'. Although the word 'God' is almost never used, God is deeply present in his works.

Much of the time Ku Sang adopts a light, amused tone, combined with deep meaning; thus he finds use even for the polluted aspect of many modern rivers as an image of the soiled inner man. Yet there too he finds hope, as the river flows into the purer immensities of the ocean. It is in his vision of a future restoration that the Oriental and the Christian strands most strikingly unite, in Ku Sang's Resurrection hope.

The word that best expresses Ku Sang's response to suffering must be 'compassion', that feeling for others which also involves suffering with them. There is little or nothing of the moralizing denunciations sometimes wrongly associated with the 'prophetic' voice. For Ku Sang, Christianity, in particular the person of Jesus of Nazareth, is the key to the hidden mystery within daily reality. It is that vision which allows him to celebrate the minute events of daily life, or confront the concrete realities of social and political wrongs without despair. That same mystery is also expressed in the more Oriental language of vast emptiness, the Void which is yet Fullness.

In the end, the impression we gain from Ku Sang's verse is that of a man intrigued to find himself alive, inexhaustibly surprised by all the things that each day reveals, delighted too by the many ways in which they can be expressed.

He has always been confronted with the fact of Western culture, with the way it challenges the Orient by its power and its sheer heaviness. No Oriental writer can avoid this. Ku Sang sometimes expresses the confrontation between East and West by setting side by side the image of Man found in Rodin's 'Thinker' and the image found in that most beautiful of all ancient Buddhist sculptures, the Maitreya carved in wood now in Kyoto but so clearly Korean in origin. As he says, who would choose to be so overwhelmed with problems when there is the possibility of such incomparable lightness?

Translator's Note

Having made a remark to the effect that it would be interesting to translate some Korean poems into English, I found myself introduced by Professor Kim Tae-Ok, the head of the English Department at Sogang University, Seoul, to the works of Ku Sang. My first thanks must go then to her, for her introduction. Many other thanks, too, for I have had to turn to her constantly for guidance about the meaning of words, indeed of whole poems. Whatever value these poems have as translations must be largely thanks to her, the errors being all my own. Her long acquaintance with Ku Sang means that I have also to thank Professor Kim for having enabled me to meet him personally. Thanks then are due to Ku Sang himself, for his delicacy, his welcome, and his simple trust. His tactful modesty I had already sensed from his poems, and his humour, but it was a particular joy to experience them directly.

Particular thanks are due to the Korean Culture and Arts Foundation; without their most generous support, this edition would not have been possible. Thanks to them, a truly representative selection of the works of a major contemporary Korean poet thus becomes available in English. A French translation of most of these poems by Roger Leverrier was published in 1986 in Paris, with a preface by René Tavernier. It is to be hoped that other similar publications may follow, so that the world at large can hear what fine songs are sung in corners of this wonderful, tragic land.

暗 称

Mystery

Myself

It is more than
the deep roots of every emotion,
big or small, of every kind,
that squirm and kick like little children
somewhere inside

and more than
the deep-sea fish
of six senses and seven sins,
that waves its tail
like a night-time shadow on a window pane

more, too, than
star-dust littering the yards
of Original Sin and Karma,
passing through the obscure darkness of the potter's kiln

and more than
the oasis spring gushing from the desert sand,
melting again into foam and flowing
after filtering through strata of origins and time
with their rustle of dry grass,
and the crack in the glacier, or even exploding particles

more, too, than
the world, itself smaller
than a millet seed
in the cosmic vastnesses

and more than
the ether — fullness of the boundless void
reaching beyond billions of light years
of starlight

more, too, than
the substantiality such fullness gives,
and more than its opposing nihility,
more, too, than unknown death

more, greater,
a soundless cosmic shout!
An immensity embracing Eternity!

Myself.

나

내 안에 四肢를 버둥거리는
어린애들처럼
크고 작은 喜怒哀樂의 뿌리
그보다도

미닫이에 밤 그림자 같이
꼬리를 휘젖는 六根이나 七罪의
深海魚보다도
옹기굴 속 無明을 지나
原罪와 業報의 마당에
널려 있는 宇宙塵보다도

또다시 거품으로 녹아 흐르고
마른 풀 같이 바삭거리는
原初와 시간의 지층을 빠져 나가서
사막에 치솟는 샘물과
氷河의 균열, 오오 粒子의 破裂!
그보다도

廣漠한 우주 안에
좁쌀알보다, 작게 떠 있는
지구보다도

億兆光年의 별빛을 넘은
虛漠의 바다에
충만해 있는 에테르보다도
그 충만이 주는 具有보다도
그 반대의 虛無보다도
未知의 죽음보다도

보다 더 큰
우주 안의 소리 없는 절규!
영원을 안으로 품은 尨大!

나.

3

Meditation

On the gleaming flank of an age-old rock,
lying like the eggs of some green insect,
fresh green moss is growing.

Is it just an effect of the springtime rain
that germinates the grain?
Or is it a return of infancy
in this centuries-old stone?

Here and now is an inevitable condition
where flowers, fruit,
and leaves too, are useless,
neither winds and rain,
nor thunder and lightning
are heard,
without distinction of day and night,
and knowing nothing of stench and perfume,
no separation of past, and reality,
and dream.

Within the rock, no flow of filth, but
the brightness of a paper window in the morning sunlight!
In its communion with heaven's vastness,
accepting all the chaos of this world's variety-show,
by simply sitting there in silent meditation
it stills the ocean's tumult.

'But I am no Aladin's lamp!'

Ah, moss so prudently clinging
to the indifferent rock!
True image of Meditation!

Here and there

A turnip field on a mountainside.
Around an ancient, springtime-drowsy rock
a single blowfly buzzes.

It comes and goes, all the time,
among old, panlid-like pats of dung
that lie in the grass on the crestward path,
now perching low on the rock's shaded waist,
now squatting high on its sunburned brow,
now moistening itself at the stagnant water
held in deep pits on its rocky crown,

then delicately folding its legs in prayer,
depositing spots of pustular waste
or laying tiny, nit-like eggs,

then flying off to land on a spring chrysanthemum's
                                        stamens,
a single red spot in the midst of the turnip field,
and there, like a little boy hypnotized by a cinema screen,
stares down at fields, rivers, roads,
as they stretch out level to the far horizon

and suddenly the world seems all suspended,
like a green, dead body,
a moment without the sound of breathing,
a moment delivered from starvation, disdain and
                                        slaughter,
this moment, without curses or conspiring,

and somehow, blowfly, dungfly,
as if for you this stillness
bred a grieving fear,
echoing, your buzzing seems to weep.

Within Creation

Beneath the garden fence,
all round the storage platform,
the rose moss blooms.

With multi-coloured stamens
crowning the soft white stems
they flirt there, posing,
nudging and jostling,
rubbing their cheeks, they bloom.

The water-melon moon
is perched high in the sky;
the night, nearly spent, is moist with dew,
and tiny butterflies come visiting,
no larger than the brooch
on my younger daughter's breast,
they hover lightly over the stamens,

yellow,
red,
pink,
green,
violet,
purple,

these butterflies, flitting from stamen to stamen
in pollen quest!
Swarms of butterflies, since spring began,
even by night, flying innumerable!

Thus bringing colours to the rainbow flowers
over thousands of years, how huge a task
these tiny things have performed, to be sure!

Behind the shed soft persimmons hang red
which, before autumn came,
would scorch and shrivel your mouth;
on the hill above, the chestnuts, too,

having bristled with spines to keep strangers at bay,
now that the nuts are ripe
and shine ready to fall,
open their mouths of their own accord.

Ah, every creature, every one,
knows the meaning of here, and tomorrow,
and so they live in togetherness,
assisting each other with all their hearts;
so how is it that I, a man, stand here
this night, all alone, like a rotting stick in a fence,
understanding nothing?

In a winter orchard

In the orchard white with snow
like sprinkled salt,
a plum tree raises thick black branches
in a victory sign,
outlined with flowers in full bloom,
like an Easter garland.

'Behold, whoever puts his life in me,
even though he dies, will never die;
do not be doubtful
of invisible realities.'

Playfully, a single magpie
hops from branch to branch.

*

Beside a hole gaping
like a cavity in a lung,
stiff as a corpse
an apple tree lies, a full arm's girth.

A man comes by, dark as shade,
with a frame bound upon his back;
he lops the dead branches with an axe,
splits the trunk, and bears it all away.

'Behold a figure of the dead
who will tomorrow be cast
into perdition's flames;
beware, then, lest the roots of your existence
become infected!'

A crow flies cawing
across the frozen sky.

Mystery

On the carpet spread in the prison cell,
so large that it fills the whole design,
a golden sunflower blazes.

Beyond the octagonal window
the city surges like ocean waves,
with factory-warships and high-rise steamers,
to say nothing of the slum shack cockle-boats.

In the sky, hovering over the city
as if attached to a cord,
a great black bat flies,
leading her young,
while in the room a naked man,
kneeling, opens wide his mouth,
about to devour a yellow butterfly
caught between his finger and thumb.

In the looking-glass built into one wall
a third man, like the other's reflection,
is dancing open-mouthed
in pursuit of another butterfly
while in the opposite wall a barred window,
edged with sharp knives,
looks out onto a sheer cliff
where a single flower is blooming.

Within this Mystery, my image
is weeping beautifully
toward a light that offers no salvation.

Midday Prayer

Take away this darkling veil
    that lies between myself and space.
Take away all boundary lines, all fences
    and all walls from every land.
Take away all human hatred,
    greed, and all discrimination.
Take away surrender and despair,
    both mine and theirs.

Restore again to me the gift of wonder, tears and prayer.
Restore again the dreams and loves of all the dead.
Restore again the hurts that human hands inflict on Nature.

And grant words to that rock, a face to this breeze,
and oh, to me grant eternal life
as a radiancy of purity.

Within an apple

Within a single apple's sphere
the clouds drift by.

Within a single apple's sphere
the good earth breathes.

Within a single apple's sphere
the river flows along.

Within a single apple's sphere
the sun blazes down.

Within a single apple's sphere
moon and stars whisper.

And within a single apple's sphere
our striving and our loving live eternal.

A pebble

On the path before my house
every day I meet a pebble
that once was kicked by my passing toe.

At first we just casually
brushed past each other, morning and night,
but gradually the stone began to address me
and furtively reach out a hand,
so that we grew close, like friends.

And now each morning the stone,
blooming inwardly with flowers of Grace,
gives me its blessing,
and even late at night
it waits watchfully to greet me.

Sometimes, flying as on angels' wings
it visits me in my room
and explains to me the Mystery of Meeting,
reveals the immortal nature of Relationship.

So now, whenever I meet the stone,
I am so uncivilized and insecure
that I can only feel ashamed.

Concerning secret joys

Children!
Let us imagine this place where I am strolling
to be a magpie's nest
up in the branches of an old plum tree!

Ah! You reckon I am living in a fool's paradise
and it makes you laugh out loud;
yet I have things to tell, no exaggeration,
more than any hero has.

Nowadays, Time and I
have grown indifferent to one another;
the wave-tossed world before my eyes,
this charivari of living and dying,
all is reduced to a distant reverberation
like snow by moonlight,
all human sympathies reconciled.

Children!
As I feast fresh, at break of day,
upon dawn's splendour spread along the branches
or upon the stillness of an evening twilight,
you simply cannot know
such joy as I experience then:
Fate made to correspond with feeling.

You simply cannot know
such happy pain.

具常無常

Impermanent I

Comic dialogue

Darling!
Don't you know?
The thing I'm looking for,
you don't know?

Don't even you know?
The thing I'm looking for now,
that thing, I don't know what it is,
that's the thing I mean!

And you say you can read my thoughts
even with your eyes closed!
That thing I've been looking for all my life,
what is it?
Don't you know?
Darling!

White lotus

In the wastelands of my heart,
sprung up unknown to man or beast,
is one white lotus plant.

In my desert-thirsty heart,
alas, why has this bud sprung up?
For now it should bloom, but it finds no way,
this white lotus flower.

Although I anxiously watch all night,
you have no wall to shield you from harm:
suppose the urchins pluck you away?
I could only suffer, frozen, dumb.

Passers-by, coveting you,
may carry you off, root and all;
I ought to prevent that, but have no means,
bud in my heart of a white lotus flower.

If you had simply never sprung up at all,
I would not have cared, most special flower;
but now, when I see you near by or afar,
the lids of the eyes of my soul inflame.

Gingko trees – a song of our marriage

Here I stand.
Turned towards you
who steadfastly wait for me,
standing there; so too I stand here.

Now is quite unlike sweet dreamland,
no response to kisses and tickling, at all;
but as we have put down deep roots of submission
into the ground of this generous loving,
you and I stand face to face.

Days and months, passing, leave in us rings of the years;
with the seasons, dreams ripen between every leaf,
then scatter,

while we simply bear fruit,
yours and mine,
as we stand for a lifetime
face to face.

Certain touching memories

After one group meditation session
we had a break for relaxation
in the shade of the convent grove
where a statue of the Virgin stood.

A delicately ageing lady of the parish
came and sat beside me on a log bench; she began:
'The region near Songdowon, that is where I am from!
Forty years ago, the mere sight of you
passing down the road in front of our yard
was enough to make me loose my senses,
and the memory has lasted a whole lifetime.
Oh, I met a nice reliable husband,
have encountered no great problems in life,
I have had several children and now
I have grandchildren too,
but your image has never faded.
Whenever I saw your name or your picture in the press
my heart would always beat faster for joy.
I have got, and read, all you have ever written.
And if I now go to church,
that too is by your example.
Of course, I know it must be embarrassing for you
to hear this kind of crazy talk;
but I did so want, just once in my life,
to meet you and tell you all these things!'
she said, and gracefully lowered her eyes.

I could find no reply;
'Perhaps, if you had only said this before . . .'
I joked.

'I could scarcely anticipate how lightly
you would take it,' she promptly retorted, to my relief.
We looked at each other, and beamed broadly.

At that moment came the sound of the assembly bell,
so side by side, like an elderly couple,
we duly made our way to the chapel.

Touching sights

Touched by an autumn afternoon's pale sunlight,
on the piano keyboard lid
lies a pair of stockings.

They must have been left there
by my daughter who is living abroad,
when she was leaving this morning.

Seeing this still-life composition, so strange
yet so completely familiar,
after fumbling and groping in my memories:

In Taegu, down a narrow lane behind the herb market,
opening my eyes in a singing-girl's room one morning
and, laid on a chest beside my pillow,
two stocking slippers come to mind.

At the same moment I begin to murmur
a phrase from a poem by O Il-Do:
'On a tree's bare branch her basket hangs,
where then has my darling gone?'

Komo Station, Mother's Station

Whenever I pass Komo Station,
my mother is waiting.
Out in front of the garden gate, she is waiting,
looking scarcely older than my wife looks now,
looking as she did the day she saw me off
when I crossed the 38th Parallel,
out in the lane, she is waiting.

Living helter-skelter, day by day,
rattling the empty lunch-box in my satchel,
coming home from school by train, as in childhood,
so now when my hair is as grey
as my father's was when he died,
out by the station she is waiting.

My mother, who stayed behind
alone in our North Korean home,
alive still, or dead, I don't know,
has come here now and is waiting.

Note: Komo is on the outskirts of Taegu, South Korea, and its name
means 'Mother-caring, Mother-recollecting'.

An autumn sickroom

In the autumn sky
flocks of wild geese fly away.
Casting long shadows
over my aching heart,
northwards they fly.
Each seems to hold the other's tail
as in straight lines they fly away.

Flapping
      flapping
           flapping
               flapping
                    flapping
                        flapping
                            flapping
                              flapping
they drop down and settle in the cavities in my breast.
                                   do
                            re
                      mi
                fa
           sol
     la
ti

the last one
I captured.

Throb
throb
throb
my heart is racing
    honk
    honk
    honk
my heart is weeping
    honk
    honk

```
        honk
the sky is weeping
            honk
honk
I set it free.
```

That single, lonely, flying form
is like me.

In the autumn sky
flocks of wild geese fly away,
within my heart
in parallel lines they fly away.

Impermanent I

Nowadays, in that world of other people
that flows away like Time,
my once panting breath subsides,
and even repentance grows faint in my breast.

As I tread on my shadow,
now more real than myself,
and stand aimlessly
like a reed waving in a dream,
and from a hole in my worn pocket
hopes and memories leak away,
fag ends and loves drop away,
bit by bit everything falls away,

no drug or drink to drown things in,
alone, awake, I stand.
Nothing matters at all.

News of death

This spring
news of a friend's death
came twice within three days.

The ones we love and miss go first.

A poet's income being what it is,
I avoid funerals.

Whenever I stand before someone dead
I feel it's my turn next.

But nothing at all is ready.

My life has been far too unfaithful,
I have failed my family
and the world too much.

And when I enter the other world,
I shall be ashamed to meet parents or neighbours.

And then, towards God
I feel nothing but dread.

Yet news of my death
cannot be long in coming.

Rehearsal for a death-bed scene

Lying under a white sheet,
I am carried off in an ambulance.

The evening sky hangs upside-down beneath my feet,
forming a terrible quagmire of death.

I picture my corpse like this, rigid, stretched out,
my skeleton, decomposed, reduced to bones.

Behind me, a lifetime lies smothered in error,
I have not even managed to bear buds of sweat and tears,
let alone the love that can blossom in Eternity.

No point in getting flustered now . . .

'Father, into your hands
I commend my spirit.'

Instinctively repeating the last words of Him
whom I have only aped, not truly served,
I sever the link with all concepts.

And my breath becomes rasping.

Old age

Here we are in no desert land.

It is rather a fresh field, nurturing mysterious buds
that will only blossom in Eternity's land.

In youth we tended to wield our bodies
but now we must use strength of mind,
and as we rouse up our sleepy souls
we must apply our attention to metaphysical things.

Above all, let us not be slaves to spectres of loneliness,
not experience cares and concerns as distractions.

Loneliness and insecurity are graces
announcing the birth of a new dimension;
using now the body's ageing, and the lack of energy,
as stimuli offered to the mind,
let us advance towards life's true renewal.

The less the joys of the flesh become,
the clearer we see both life and self;
so, as the flames of faith, hope, and love burn brighter,
let us listen more closely to Eternity's voice.

Now let us awake from this illusory dream
where, like the leaves and blossoms of Nature,
everything blooms to vanish with the seasons,

and cherishing a glorious, undying dream
that will bloom beyond death, on another shore,
let us live an old age as radiant as silver.

드레퓌스의
벤취에서

From
Dreyfus'
Bench

On suffering

They come storming on. Stones fly.
The boys wield dung-bound millet stalks,
the older men swing hoes as on they come in rough
                                                    pursuit,
I turn and stand, tears trickling down,
sheltering a brow from which blood thickly oozes,
no sign of mother's face here,
where can I run to now?

Pursued and again pursued, I hid.
In the hut where they keep the hearse, I hid.
Insults, deep disgrace, shouts of anger,
round and round like a swarm of bees they turned
while I quickly pushed open the lid of the hearse,
jumped in, lay down, held my breath.

My breast grew cool, as after coughing blood,
my heart grew light, as after drinking wine;
within the hearse, that neither man nor ghost dares
                                                    approach,
I found myself weaving a scene from a sweet dream.
The face of one resting like a corpse in a hearse,
must seem white as the full moon itself.
A girl, sly as the harvest moon, eyes twinkling stars,
seemed to be pouring sweet oil upon my wounds:
a dream within my sweet dream.

And by the pond of memory
a single lotus flower of love seemed to bloom.
That other love was riven to loneliness,
she stood there alone, like a statue, a log,
having discarded her scarlet shoes.

Riding the hearse, bright as a cartload of flowers,
and following the road towards Limbo,
even the noise of keening is joyful!
Ah, my darling in mourning white,
only wait for the third day to come.

Dawning

In the sky, now brightening to the East,
a crow passes.

As night is about to give way to dawn,
this street, as sinister as the Casbah,
is haunted by deep shadows,
a dreadful alley . . .

but then,
to the sound of a drum-beat,
the citadel gates, thick with moss of resentment,
creak open, and along the street,
venom-spread like a serpent's back,
a torch-bearing Sibyll rides, crying 'Awake!'
from a white courser's back.

Trampling of hooves, trampling of hooves,
clashing of spears and swords,
the screams of peoples
ready for slaughter
fill the air.

And as the sun rises,
a man vomits blood and dies
— his smile radiant.

Addition to Exodus

You know, in those days too they made
a golden calf and worshipped it.

Trust, sincerity of love,
such basic necessities of existence,
thrown aside like old sticks or worn-out boots,
they became beasts,
fighting one another, simply wearing human masks.

The world, with Aaron's hoardes in charge,
became a place of submissiveness.

But even then there were people
trusting, waiting for Moses to come down from Sinai,
simply, in solitude.

Ah, Canaan,
flowing with milk and honey!
Ah, far off and how hard to reach.

Vested with Moses'
foresight and wrath

Vested with Moses' foresight and wrath, I speak:
If this new year you would return to truly human living,
you must first get rid
of the golden calf you now adore:

If you would banish from your table all harmful foodstuffs,
    first you must get rid of that golden calf
and if you hope to put an end to air-pollution in your city,
    first you must get rid of that golden calf
and if you aim to abolish discord in your household,
    first you must get rid of that golden calf
and if you desire harmony with brethren and neighbours,
    first you must get rid of that golden calf
and if you are to save little children from dying in accidents,
    first you must get rid of that golden calf
and if you intend to keep marital fidelity,
    first you must get rid of that golden calf
and if you wish to avoid daylight murder and robbery,
    first you must get rid of that golden calf
and if you would prevent slaughter on land and sea,
    first you must get rid of that golden calf
and if you hope to see eternal truths taught and learned
                        at school
    first you must get rid of that golden calf
and if you look to be treated and healed in hospitals,
    first you must get rid of that golden calf
and if you expect the law to protect you with its justice,
    first you must get rid of that golden calf
and if you intend to reduce the gap between rich and poor,
    first you must get rid of that golden calf
and if you intend to escape mutual indifference and
                        rejection,
    first you must get rid of that golden calf
and if you do not want the curse of another civil war,
    first you must get rid of that golden calf
and if you want to reconcile in a peaceful heart
                     dreams and actions,

if you would venerate once again the fruits
of invisible strength and life bestowed by such things
                                as Eternity, faith or love,
    first you must get rid of that golden calf.

Vested with Moses' foresight and wrath, I speak:
If this new year you wish to live purely, impeccably,
you must get rid of the golden calf you now adore.

Shame

In the zoo,
peering between bars and netting,
I search for an animal
that knows what shame is.

I say, keeper!
Might there just possibly be
in those monkeys' red posteriors
at least some trace of it?

What of the bear's paw, perpetually licked?
Or the seals' whiskers,
or maybe the parrot's beak?
Is there really no trace of it there?

Since shame has vanished
from the people of this city,
I've come to the zoo to look for it.

From Dreyfus' Bench –
Convict Jean's soliloquy

Papillon! Now the evening sea is nothing but a rocking darkness, but how could I ever forget the image of you drifting away on a coconut raft, even though I die and pass to the other world!

Papillon! If I did not go away with you, it was not at all because I was afraid of being found out by the guards and getting lashed, or of being eaten by sharks or dolphins and becoming a sea-spirit, and it was not from a dread that your seventh escape would fail too and we would be hauled back together.

Papillon! Before you left, I could never have told you this, but I have realized that, even supposing there really is a promised land waiting with open arms to welcome us when we reach the mainland, there is no new life for us. You see, I have come to realize that this world is all a prison, no matter where you go, and that all people without exception are convicts in it. I have realized that a life spent under the fierce glares of the guards who watch over this 'Island of Death', and getting along with all the dangerous ruffians housed in our cell, while raising the 200 pigs I am in charge of, that such a life is no better and no worse than life anywhere else in the world.

Papillon! Therefore the freedom that you are leaving here in search of, looks to me just like shackles. I feel that in this world there is no land without barred windows and chains, visible or invisible, there is only that freedom which we make our life's domain within ourselves and which transforms every kind of bond into our own loving and yearning.

Papillon! Having come to see all this, I let you go off alone, and now I am so very lonely.

Note: In Henri Charrière's *Papillon*, Dreyfus' Bench is the name given to a bench on the clifftop of the Island of Death, the penal colony. Jean is a Chinese prisoner who befriends the main character but refuses to escape with him.

Weeping of magpies

On the roof of Seoul City Hall,
mapgies in a cage, earlier than others
show weepy eyes.
Partly on account of the all-pervading exhaust fumes,
but mainly they weep
because their present life is so awful.

Pecking at the grain that is regularly scattered,
                              they weep
Sipping the water in a bowl, they weep.
Watching the pigeons in the square fly up and down,
                              they weep.
Looking across to the distant hills,
seeing the trees in the near-by park, they weep.
Watching the cars lined up nose-to-tail, they weep.
Beholding the activities of the people coming and going,
                              they weep
Seeing at times the source of all authority appear,
                              they weep.
Huddled at night in artificial nests, they weep.
Looking up by night at the stars in the sky, they weep.
Recalling the past, they weep.
Imagining the future, they weep.
And if they consider the chicks
that hatch and grow up in their cage,
tears pour down.

On the roof of Seoul City Hall,
magpies in a cage, earlier than others,
show weepy eyes.

Back from Vietnam

After vain efforts to decipher
this message, a single page
that fluttered down from somewhere,
I have returned.

In the shade of palm trees at Kumong Pass,
beside the sea at Vongtau,
even sitting with aodai-clad bargirls
in Saigon,
I strove to decipher it, in vain;
I have returned.

It might be propaganda
dropped by the Vietcong. I am not sure.

Or a trick by a Vietnamese child
I met at Natrang orphanage. I am not sure.

Maybe it is a ploy of some secret service,
to test my way of thinking. I am not sure.

It might be a poster
of the Pope's appeal for peace. I am not sure.

Or perhaps, rather, it may be a last will and testament
left by one of our Korean heroes. I am not sure.

You see, it was
in the form of a falling tear.

You see, it was
in the form of prison fetters.

You see, it was
in the form of a hole
pierced by a falling shell.

You see, it was
in the form of a limbless skeleton.

Or rather, it was
in the shape of a bitter spirit unable to find rest.

Yet it seemed
to be something to do with Vietnam.

Yet it also seemed
to be something concerning me in particular.

Yet it also seemed
to concern my fellow-countrymen.

But it seemed mainly
to be a strong suggestion
aimed at all the peoples of the world.

And the only thing that I have felt
thanks to it
is that I as an individual,
that indeed the whole of humanity,
we are all still utterly ignorant. Only that.

So now, still unable
to really decipher the message,
since I have managed to return,
I publish it like this.

On a sheet of white paper
traced in red blood
a question-mark:

　　　?

What can it mean?

Homeward journey

On board Gemini 6,
the rendez-vous completed,
on the way back down,
just as in the evening
farmers return homeward
riding on oxen
and playing willow flutes,

eating one mouthful less of steak
(to reduce his weight)
then pulling out the harmonica
hidden in an arm pocket
and making music, oomp-pa-pa,
eager to be home with wife and kids,
he sailed back down earthwards.

The pen

As a drop of dew penetrates the ground
then issues as a springing source,
with that same limpid energy
let us wield the pen.

As men set fire to dense forests
then till the wild and create new fields,
with that same fertile vision
let us wield the pen.

With all the arduous sweat of the miner
piercing rock a thousand feet below
let us wield the pen.

With all the precision and care
of the surgeon's scalpel in an open heart
let us wield the pen.

With reasoned thought
bright as the snow on high mountains,
with the dexterity of soldiers
checking front-line positions,
with the slave's resolve and determination
as he breaks his irons with his bare teeth,
overcoming discouragement and despair
like Sisyphus,

vested with a love
that weeps even to see
a new-sprung weed trampled on,
with the spiritual poverty of a Paek-Kyol,
let us wield the pen.

Note: Paek Kyol, literally 'Hundred Patches' was a famous scholar
renowned for his great poverty and integrity.

신령한
새싹

Mysterious
Buds

In all places

Are you within such stillness
as when, above a shimmering pond,
a dreamlike butterfly gently descends?

Are you obscurely there
in the desolate hills under rain,
their secluded places wrapped in darkness?

Are you like the compassion
appearing in hillside temple courts
where a flowering plantain's leaves
shelter a single rose-moss flower?

Are you found forlorn
beneath the bright hanging moon,
like shadows cast by a rooftop terrace?

Are you in some such height
as where chains of blue-tinged peaks
rise like screens around,
but above towers one snow-bright?

Are you in such perfect composure
as the long river timelessly flowing,
reflecting the sun and the moon?

Are you in the transparent frost
that unfolds on chill autumn mornings,
coating the naked branches?

Are you within that abundance
that undulates in the fields,
gold in the setting sun's slanting rays?

Are you too reduced to original silence,
like the soil ravaged by long winter's cold,
all fever spent?

Are you in such solemn power
as when the typhoon surges
and tidal waves race,
with clashes of lightning and thunder?

Are you as far removed
as the blending of vast blue immensity,
sea and sky made one
beyond all boundlessness?

Are you resplendent
as daybreak in the eastern sky,
high above the sevenfold rainbow's gleam,
like constellations' jewelled thrones?

Are you within the inborn joy
of swarms of fish flashing in jade-green streams
and the birds that chirp
while plum and peach delicately bloom?

Are you in the impassibility
of the mountain sheep
that nibbles grass then chews the cud,
looking up now at a cloud, now at a hill?

Are you in such spotless innocence
as shines in the eyes of a child
that gazes up at its mother and clasps
her breast through an open blouse?

Are you looking down on us
with the profound white-bearded smile
of drawings of Taoist Mountain Wizards?

You who fill all space and time,
whom I cannot serve under any such forms
but who resemble the white spaces in pictures
where the brush did not pass!

In no place confined,
by nothing defined,
everywhere present,
Lord God of all!

To John

John! My slow-witted friend!
Have you still not understood that perfect joy
would not be in you, even if having written poems
bright as the sun on a New Year's morning
you enjoyed world-wide fame?

John! My slow-witted friend!
Have you still not understood that perfect joy
would not be in you, even if you were to marry Miss World
and live in rooms spread with rich cushions
and supplied with ten thousand books,
sitting down three times a day to delicious meals?

John! My slow-witted friend!
Have you still not understood that perfect joy
would not be in you, even if you were adored and revered
by your sons and daughters, while you lived entranced
by the cute antics of all your little grandchildren?

Ah, John! You old leper soul!
Why, if you want to find true joy welling up within you,
well, you may realize one day that everything
in your present life is a source of mystery
and you may come to feel gratitude for so many
undeserved gifts; therefore your brother, Francis of Assisi,
exclaimed: 'If the Lord were to take from me
all the grace he has bestowed, and give it to thieves
                                        instead,
he would receive my sincerest thanks.'

As he walked alone

I must walk alone.
As he walked alone
two thousand years ago under Roman rule,
to the insults of Scribes and Pharisees,
so I too must walk alone.

Among luxuriant gardens of evil,
although the truth is sad and hard,
although I often taste the bitter cup of failure,
exhausted in lonely helplessness,
just as he walked alone along the Way of the Cross,
betrayed, abandoned by the disciples,
with people mocking and throwing stones,
so I too must walk alone.

Trusting that justice will triumph, eternal,
trusting that suffering accepted has value,
trusting that our love and hope are not vain,

not putting on heroic airs,
with nothing to show but a cripple's grace,
just as he walked alone on the way of Resurrection,
so I too must walk alone.

Christmas lament

Ah, venerable Church!
With none of the simple joys of those shepherds
who came first of all
to worship around your crib!
With nothing left of the peace of your stable.

fearing the coming of your kingdom,
tonight too Herod and his henchmen keep watch,
ready to lop off your young shoots,
keeping Christmas with glaring eyes.

And your disciples,
changing the colour of the Gospel
like a beaded dress displayed in a shop window,
the colour varying with the lighting,
with the enthusiastic mob,
and the Pharisees, today too,
all crowd around
you;

and like Zacchaeus perched in a tree,
one crow-like soul cries:
'On me and on all held in cursed bondage
turn, oh turn your eyes!'

Easter hymn

On an old plum tree stump,
seemingly dead and rotten,
like a garland of victory
flowers gleam, dazzling.

Rooted in you, even in death
all things remain alive;
we see them reborn, transfigured.
How then could we doubt
our own Resurrection since
by your own you gave us proof?

Since there is your Resurrection and ours,
    Truth exists;
since there is your Resurrection and ours,
    Justice triumphs;
since there is your Resurrection and ours,
    suffering accepted has value;
since there is your Resurrection and ours,
    our faith, hope, love, are not in vain;
since there is your Resurrection and ours,
    our lives are not an empty abyss.

In this lost corner of the earth,
dappled by the spreading spring,
as I imagine that Day's world,
made perfect by our Resurrection,
I am overwhelmed in rapture.

Before the Virgin's statue

Your sweetness, Holy Mother,
comes rising from the lily of the valley!

Held down by your pretty bare feet,
coiled flat on top of the earthly globe,
not at all ill at ease, with eyes half shut
the serpent dozes and shrugs.

Shedding as it passes by
a strong smell of fresh green barley
slyly the spring breeze stirs
your skirts and the deep blue belt;
with your white veil,
your eyes that scan the skies
hold a gleam of vague resentment.

Beyond this nation's celadon skies,
beyond deep gulfs of vast nothingness,
can you glimpse from here
the Kingdom of Jesus your son
who went away, leaving in your silken breast
the wounds of the Seven Sorrows?

This May afternoon,
as I kneel with hands joined
in the shadow of the cliff at Lourdes,
all things are breathing regularly.

Mysterious buds

The pitiless whirlwinds
have blown themselves out, and within me
mysterious buds have begun to grow.

What then is this freshness
touching my gaunt senses
that were dry as winter acacia trees?

All the things of creation,
once plunged in darkness,
turn into stars
and twinkling, begin to shine;
until now locked in a tangled mesh,
my ideas flow free like thread from a skein.

Now there is nothing sad for me
about being born only to die;
all is just one aspect of eternity.

I still feel hungry if a meal is delayed,
my limbs still have rheumatic twinges,
nothing has changed, but within me

mysterious buds have begun to grow,
preparing to bloom with new flowers
once in Eternity's land.

Mysterious wealth

Feeling today like the Prodigal Son
just arrived back in his father's arms,
I observe the world and all it contains.

June's milky sky glimpsed through a window,
the sunlight dancing over fresh green leaves,
clusters of sparrows that scatter, chirping,
full-blown petunias in pots on verandas,
all strike me as infinitely new,
astonishing and miraculous.

My grandson, too, rushing round the living-room
and chattering away for all he's worth,
my wife, with her glasses on,
embroidering a pillow-case,
and the neighbours, each with their particularities,
coming and going in the lane below,
all are extremely lovable,
most trustworthy, significant.

Oh, mysterious, immeasurable wealth!
Not to be compared with storeroom riches!
Truly, all that belongs to my Father in Heaven,
all, all is mine!

The true appearance of the Word

As the cataract of ignorance falls
from off the eyesight of my soul,
I realize that all this huge Creation
round about me is the Word.

The hitherto quite unattended fact
that these familiar fingers number ten,
like an encounter with some miracle,
suddenly astonishes me

and the newly-opened forsythia flowers
in one corner of the hedge beyond my window
entrance me utterly,
like seeing a model of Resurrection.

Smaller than a grain of sand
in the oceanic vastness of the cosmos,
I realize that this my muttering,
by a mysterious grace of the Word,

is no imagined thing, no mere sign,
but Reality itself.

Jesus of Nazareth

Jesus of Nazareth!
Who are you really?

Born in a stable's manger,
dying nailed to a cross with thieves,
the unlucky possessor of an absurd destiny.

Wandering around, without house or home,
you kept company with low class people,
with prostitutes and rebels,
with louts from other regions
normally considered enemies;
you enjoyed eating and drinking with them.

To the poor,
to the hungry,
to those in tears,
to those despised for their just deeds,
insulted, driven out, and dishonoured
for having practised what is right,
you dared to proclaim:
'You, you are the blessed!
Yours, yours is the Kingdom of God!'

You gave sight to the blind,
you opened the deaf man's ears,
you made the cripple walk,
you completely healed the leper's sores,
you brought the dead back to life,

as you yourself said,
heaped with the whole world's hatred,
insulted and driven out,
finally labelled a traitor
and dying without any show,
you are the ultimate failure

and to me, united with you from my mother's womb,
you are the very ground of my being, the way
from which, at times, I incline to stray,
finding it a nuisance,
at times a cause of discouragement, despair;
at times, although extremely familiar,
you look like an absolute stranger.

*

So what on earth are you really like?
You weren't a thinker,
you weren't a moralist,
you weren't one of this world's statesmen,
and you weren't the founder of a religion.

Therefore, you didn't teach any kind of learning,
you didn't teach any kind of rules,
you didn't launch any kind of social reform movement,
neither did you teach some kind of detachment from
                                                  this world.

You didn't compute
anyone's past merit, or lack of it,
you didn't compute
anyone's past sins, whether many or few.
Really, you overturned the thoughts and words
of everyone in the world:
'Come to me, all you
who are toiling and struggling along
under heavy burdens,
I will give you rest!'
To suffering humanity
you proclaimed liberation,

and you taught that God is our Father,
that he is Love itself, infinite,
that when, nestling like children in his breast,
we forgive as our Father forgives,
and love as our father loves,

then eternal bliss dwells in our lives,
and that, you taught, is called 'the Kingdom of God'
and having practised at the cost of your life
the sincerity of such loving,
you bore witness by your Resurrection
to that Love's imperishability.

초생달
꽃밭

Garden

by

Moonlight

Springtime dances

The old plum tree stump,
wimpled in white,
is dancing the dance of the crane.

The towering pine trees,
extending green parasols in either hand,
are performing a waltz.

Weeping willows sway in rhythms free,
 bony acacias
rock leafless shoulders,
while bamboos rubbing arms and legs
step it out together.

Along the wayside where snow meets the sun
tiny blades of grass, already sprouting,
gently sway.

Seeds, roots, insects, frogs,
that had only been peeping from underground windows
now put on their springtime best,
like actors in backstage dressing rooms.
Now the breath of spring in the breeze
comes gently brushing the naked flesh.

Spring washing

Along the edge of a barley field
weeping willow trees
dip their tresses in a stream.

Sunbeams beneath the water,
turned to golden grains of sand, dance
then pause, then flow again.

Hunched like toads
new crawled from the ground,
the village women and girls
attack the springtime washing.

Slip-slop, slip-slop,
tacka-tacka-tacka, slosh-slosh,
they beat away
as if pounding out the rice-cake paste.

Chick-check, chick-chock,
yick-yeck, yick-yock,
heh-heh, hee-hee! The tongues wag away:

Here's a baby girl born in the year of the horse!
The father-in-law's not too pleased about that!
and here's a mother-in-law too strict by half,
or a cheeky student for a sister-in-law,
but there a husband's gone back after leave,
and as for the gangsters of a certain political party . . .

In this pleasant scene
there still remain shadows of personal pain,
like stains in the embroideries
made by young widows.

Spring chrysanthemums

At one window of an apartment block,
in an old orange-box
with a scrap of soil
and a packet of seeds sprinkled,
spring chrysanthemums
yellow,
red,
pink,
turquoise,
white,
are spreading their petals.

Single blossoming sign of Nature
in an artificial world!

Scarcely arrived, the spring-morning sunshine
dazzles, then slips away.

At the third floor opposite, a pink blanket
waves like a tongue while the owner,
a dancer, squints across;

above, on the sixth floor, a student is listening to jazz,
brushing the dandruff from bushy hair
and staring down.

On the ground floor a bank-guard's wife,
her perm in a towel
as she fiercely beats cushions,
pauses to glance up.

And the unmarried pensioner next door,
changing the water in his goldfish-bowl,
stops and looks sideways

while the two kid brothers to the left
stop playing at housekeeping
and turn to look.

In the street a bean-curd seller,
ringing a hand-bell as he passes,
stops and looks up

and the ice-cream man,
pushing his cart along,
looks up too, wiping his brow

while the newly-married housewife
watering her flowers
cannot help thinking of her husband
whom she has just pushed off to work,
after a good number of tongue-bites,
and very slightly she smiles.

Scenes of a summer's day

1. Morning

Mountains, villages and fields,
all decked with scales of green,
dazzle the eyes,

along the far-stretching cotton-white paths
men, bursting with well-being
like those you see in the city
in advertisements for health products,
out at work since dawn
irrigating the rice-fields,
are returning homewards.

2. Noontide

A jolly lass sets out, bearing the workers' lunch
in a basket on her head,
a hairy dog trotting behind her.

Refreshed by a scoopful of makkoli,
a bowl of rice,
a moment's snooze,
the men go back to the rice fields,
while a pair of white herons
fly across the sky
with a creaking sound.

3. Evening

Through the evening twilight,
driving a cow,
with a frame on their backs, they return.

The smoke from kitchen fires,
the brushwood gate, offer warm welcome.

As from time immemorial,
hills, villages, fields,
all are unchangingly here,
and even in this land's present chaos
this primordial scene is in itself enough
to restore serenity.

Seaside in a lost homeland

First, you bathe in the blue vault of the sky
as it dips itself in the radiant sea,
then, once become pale as green vegetables,
you plough through the thunderous surf
and climb the sandy beach, spread like sackcloth,
and wallow stretched out in the scorching sun;
then, passing a fringe of flowering shrubs,
you enter the green shelter of a pine grove
and there, in its green shade,
you satisfy your healthy appetite.
Ah, my lost homeland! My lost Paradise!
Wonsan! Songdowon!

*

Above your deep blue skirts,
over your silken breasts
a white towel lies stretched
and your heart vibrates heat,
a golden light as from a furnace,
and the whole universe is glorious.
Miles of bright sand!

*

My friend, my Western friend!
Do you really think the Mediterranean,
that sea of burning strands,
can be life's ultimate shore?

No, surely not!
It is not just a matter of scorching sun and blue sea,
of white waves and sparkling strands,
for the liberation we desire is not there.

Only imagine for a moment!
In the very centre of the Pacific Ocean,
that immeasurable vastness

surging to and fro in all directions,
endless on every side;
or in the Arabian deserts, beneath a scorching sun
the suffocating tortures of thirst,
tell me, how could we ever celebrate life there?

It is a terrifying thing, you know,
but I have to have in life's primordial village
a pine grove as by my Wonsan sea shore;
and at times beneath a death-like cloud of sorrow
I must remain and rest.
My friend, my Western friend!

Moonlit evening

As the moon was bathing lazily
in the still waters of a well,
she was caught in the bucket, up she went,
was poured out into a stoneware jar.

Scooped from there in a fresh hollow gourd,
she flowed all down a bride's black hair,
over creamy back and swelling breasts,
down she slipped, and away she went,
splashing into shivers on a washing-stone.

The moon-washed flesh was now white as moon . . .

From high up on the straw-pale roof
the pepper-pods look down,
their faces blush redder than ever.

Glancing up at the moon,
now somehow back up on high,
the pumpkins are embarrassed
and shyly creep under their vines.

In the flower-beds the balsam flowers watch it all,
they see and drop petals at so much fun,
moistening their eyes with dewdrops.

Thoughts as winter comes

1. First frost

Along the branches of old trees,
stripped of every last leaf,
the hoarfrost-flowering morning cleanly spreads.

The ivory brow of the catechism sister,
object of my tiny breast's deepest childhood longing,
creeps into my mind.

Purity is no matter for melancholy, surely,
yet my eyes are moist with a chill dew.

2. First day of winter

Feebly advancing sunbeams
dragging long shadows
seek out the sunny spots.

The earth, with no fever left,
lies in its primitive state.

In this November twilight
my life, too, begins its return.

3. First snow

When the first snowfalls come,
blessings descend on the blessed
but anguish seizes the wretched.

As snow drops down pale
from the dark night sky,
the lamplit streets become silent sanctuaries

and from some distant place
a raucous sound echoes,
like the call of a boat which has lost its port.

In a winter street

The winter twilight hangs despairingly
like the tattered banner on the red brick building,
while on the roadway before a squat fence,
with strips of cement sacks in place of a sandy beach,
a few baby tortoises
lie heaped together.

The salesman stands there,
gaunt as the bare trees along the roadside,
veiled in a whitish dust,
and when his spidery hand pulls the thread it holds,
the baby tortoises scrabble, scatter,
scrabble, scrabble, scatter,
and fall off their paper shore.

Rattle, rattle, crash!
As the shutters slam down in front of the bank
a veil of darkness descends before the eyes;
a wave of people presses on, unseeing,
and with a dock-side uproar
buses screech in and away.

As the coal-black waters of a meager stream
flow unseen beneath the asphalt where he stands,
so too in the hungry innards of the salesman,
scrabble, scrabble, the turtles run
and as they run they fall.

In the lamp-light,
shining there like a lighthouse on a desert island,
the scraps of paper seem a sea-bed
viewed through a fish-eye lens,
or a tomb on which a flock
of jackdaws has settled.

In this desolate scene,
suppose the corpse of some dead wartime companion
should come up and clasp his hand,
I reckon he would weep for joy.

Eros I

A torso like a ripe peach.

A butterfly fallen
drunk in ecstasy on a flowery tomb.

A tongue with the perfume of melons.

A seagull plunging
into blue waves that flash white teeth.

In a gaze fixed on the distant horizon.

A roe deer
drinking at a secret spring in a virgin forest.

Abyss of Eros,
beauty of original sin.

Eros II

The purring cat's
deceitful, mysterious face.

Venus' neck
spun about with hempen locks.

On breasts of velvet
the imprint of a hawk's claws.

An hour-glass navel.

Buttocks the smooth bottom of a wooden bowl,
secret flesh of tree-trunk thighs.

The narrowing rapids of a rendez-vous,
a grassy bank aflame on a spring day.

In primitive darkness,
beneath an azalea-cliff blanket
a naked woman
on a foaming, lapping wave-white sheet
joins her arms
like the cords
that criminals are bound with

. . . . .

The cooing of doves.

Breath-taking moment, oh, mystic ritual!

Eros III

I draw in empty space.

That face,
that voice,
that smile,
those thighs,
but that love
cannot be drawn.

Things drawn in the heart
may not be given form.

Eros IV

With that same hand
that carressed her naked body
I stroke my grey beard.

Passion faded into pale silver . . .

That loving, riding the bucket,
has been drawn up to the heavens.
Henceforth, all those times and places
are one with Eternity.

木瓜
옹두리에도
사연이

Even the
Knots on
Quince Trees

1.

A bridled,
foaming,
drooling
cow.

Aged four, my first revelation of really existing
found in a face like that printed by blood and sweat
on a cloth held out by a Jerusalem woman
to a man on his way to execution:
the face of a cow.

The yellow, twilit path slid up over a mountainside,
calligraphic in black and white,
I gazed at the face of the cow as it plodded along the
                                    muddy track,

and while I sat there perched on the leading cart
with an ancient cupboard roped down in the wagon
                                    behind,
my first buds of knowledge unfolded,
and I wept.

2.

Could it have been
on account of long familiarity
with my cousin's embroidery frame?

My little breast
tortured with longings,
I gazed up.

Over the wimple and creamy face
of the catechism-class sister,
whistling like a train leaving for the Manchurian border,
a river was spreading wide and flowed.

I saw
the desolate back of the sun
that day, too.

3.

In Minor Seminary,
early one New Year's Day,
having cut out from the newspaper
a picture of Her Imperial Majesty
all dressed in white,
I rushed straight to the toilets.

Having done like the serpent in Genesis,
who, squirming his whole body, expelled
like pus a blasphemous passion,
I turned my back on that monastery
in which I had spent three years.

And I became a follower of isms.

4.

I began by running away.

On the night ferry to Japan,
tossing on a single tatami space,

the cabin with its owl's eye
is a miniature tunnel with no way out,
and the roar of the engines tortures my heart.

So this young man,
fettered in chains of history,
throwing aside his coat and sitting up,
turns into a nameless beast
and grinds his teeth.

Galilee with no Master!

Riding the waves of darkness,
Yun Shim-Dock with dishevelled hair in grief
hails me.

Note: Yun Shim-Dock was a Korean girl who fell in love with a Japanese
man, and, their love being hopeless since he was married, they committed
suicide together.

5.

In this enemy town, on a spring day so harmonious
it brings tears to my eyes,
with a missal
and a book called 'Wretchedness'
wedged under my arm,
all day long I wander aimlessly.

Crossing the Aragawa,
which flows towards its irreversible history,
I enter a bar in Kitashenshu
and sit squeezed between Korean labourers
to swallow down my toburoko.

'Kwejina chingching naneh!'
Who will light, who will light
this lamp, who will light?
In the midst of this dark night
who will light our lamp?
'Kwejina chingching naneh!'

Twenty years old, my first taste of drink:
on the way home, sky and streets
and people
all remind me of Van Gogh's 'Night with Stars'.

6.

At that time
the encounter with La Rochefoucauld
aroused a typhoon within me.

The early buds of eager desire to do good
vanished brutally, in a flash,
and, darkness-wrapped within,
I saw two-headed monsters come to life,
that tore at each other, roaring.

Moment by moment
the cord of self-hatred
tightened around my throat;
the silence of nature changed into horror,
other people became 'Hell'
and human existence a world of utter evil . . .

Stretched out on my boarding-house tatami floor,
I celebrated daily
funerals of God

and sitting beside a pond in Kitsijoji Park,
I imagined the rapture
of a Zarathustra
climbing up to the stronghold of the Superman.

7.

In the coffee-shop 'Etranger'
was Yumi,
a eurasian girl
with White Russian blood.

At first I pestered her
to become my little sister,
but with no success.

One evening, near midnight,
after several glasses of vodka,
when I suddenly fell on her cherry lips,
just that once she exclaimed,
'No acting like that, brother!'

The course of my love:
constantly such falsehoods,
no unity!
And a miserable conclusion.

Thirty years later, even now,
in the Shangri-la of dreams
I always feel anxious
about my encounter with Yumi.

Affection in me impotent?

8.

On my thickly growing branches
the Duino Elegies
brought out buds of pantheism.

My human life: a morning dewfall on the grass,
all things existing, hitherto mere appearance,
bringing forth light from within
and, day by day, dying.

One day, as the tears
of impermanence were brimming full,
a fountain of song
began to rise within me.

'Until that day
when my flesh becomes leaves,
my bones stalks,
and when from my scarlet blood
a bouquet of flowers shall rise,
ah, my life!'

That was the first phrase
of my first poem.

9.

Invoking Golgotha's Mother and Son,
praying so hard it parched his tongue,
still invoking, he died.

Such a death
in which this world and the world beyond
are linked by chains of pain!

With candles burning and prayers for the dead rising,
before that corpse,
moulded over my life, such pain!
And born of what seeds?
Not knowing was the worst torment.

But the torrent of that destiny
continued to flow in my veins!
Abruptly thinking to cut off that inheritance,
as I turned my face away
from my hideously stiff father,
I broke into a wail.

10.

For a while, frequenting Lao Tzu and Chuang Tzu,
I enjoyed playing with words:

empty, empty,
you must empty,
if you empty me not away,
I'll empty you away.
Play, play,
you must play,
if you play no tricks on me,
I'll play tricks on you.

Then somehow, frequenting folklore gods,
I went crazy exorcizing:

belt and shoes,
tiger, tailor,
frogs, clogs,
spinning spindle,
loom and treadle.

焦土의

詩

Wasteland
Poems

1.

Against the window panes of a wretched hovel
children's faces
press like blazing sunflowers.

They turn away, dazzled by the sun's piercing,
and I too turn away;
a moping shadow trudges behind me.

Down an alley chosen at random I pause;
in a hedge half-smothered in ashes
forsythia flowers are budding.

Down a hill a little girl comes running,
smiling a gappy smile with no front teeth,
absolutely blameless.

I cheer up like after a drink
and my shadow prances before me, grinning.

2.

I suppose that anyone would laugh if they saw someone
gently caressing a squid all black with its ink, holding it
cuddled in their lap?

But as I sat there opposite her, my eyes were hard.

'Chong-sik dear, do be still; when we find Daddy,
he will buy you sweets.'

A woman too pale by far was sitting there, almost
begging her little negroid boy to be quiet.

After midnight, on the night train, beneath the
pallid lamps the expressions of the passengers were not
at all amused; on the head of the little sobbing black boy
and the brow of his distracted mother drops of sweat
sparkled strangely.

I observe this mis-matched black-and-white picture of
mother and child, then search my pockets for a bag of
toffees a half-drunken friend forced on me as he saw me
off, and offer one to the child.

No doubt about it, the effect is instant. Blinking eyes
blacker than jet, he grabs the sweet, conveys it to his
mouth and becomes unexpectedly serious.

A second, a third, a fourth, and he comes scrambling
up into my lap, grinning happily and showing bright
white teeth.

I have no choice but to play the game. I take charge
of the child from the woman, whose eyes are tearful
behind an apologetic smile and, pulling funny faces, I
mobilize caramels and all possible talents for the task.

Things soon take an unexpected turn. More than
relieved at such unlooked-for help, surely exhausted in
mind and body, the woman quietly falls asleep. And the
child, a moment before playing wildly, no doubt feeling
that the time is right, begins to snore in my arms.

Thus transformed, with no effort on my part, into
being the father of a black child, in an indescribable state
of mind, I close my eyes too.

Inwardly I picture the few banknotes that must be the secret of this child's birth.

I think of the hillside where the father may have perished or of the medal shining on his proud homeward-bound breast, if he survived.

I sense in the face of this harrassed, overwhelmed woman what it means to be Korean today.

Holding the now quietly breathing little innocent, I shudder at the thought of the flimsy destiny awaiting him and humanity.

Meanwhile the train races on, piercing the night, the travellers all dozing exhausted; I have now become a black-and-white picture of father and son, and on my brow rise drops of sweat.

3.

On the frozen ground of my heart
a bitter Siberian wind bites the flesh.

In a field of dry tangled weeds
a garbage dump
of gaping cans, smashed ration-boxes,
pages from an Army newspaper, broken-necked bottles,
and in one corner the cadaver of a hairy dog, shot dead;
along the ridges bitten into the fields by tanks
the dry stiff carcass of a cat;
in front of a tent like a plastic hot-house
behind a barbed-wire fence hung with blood-stained
                                        slacks,
coming and going, a yankee soldier;
whenever he whistles, peep-peep,
wretched urchins pop up their heads, like frogs,
from holes in the ground like those where kimchi is kept,
wrapped in coloured scarves,
yellow, red and blue.

The sky suddenly
begins to spew black mist
and a cluster of crows flaps off
over the sullen hills.

This itch in my back that drives me mad,
this rising bile that dilates my breast,
what causes it?

4.

Scene 1

Down the street, urchins troop round a strangely-dressed girl. Some make to throw stones, others wave sticks dipped in cow pats or horse dung.

'Yankees' whore! Yankeeeees' whoooore! Yankees' whore!'

They are set to deal with sullied motherhood according to our law.

'I'm not your mother am I!? Yankees' whore indeed! What of it!'

She spits out the words from foaming lips, as a passing American jeep stops, then zooms away like the wind. Only the sound of the shouts remains.

Scene 2

A heavily made-up woman passes, in western clothes. Kids wink at one another.

One creeps up behind and skillfully fixes a sign on her back: '3000 won a trick'.

'Waha! Wahaha! Wahahaha!'

Realizing that their laughter is really pointless as resistance, the children indulge in it as a form of sadism.

The woman checks her heels, corrects her poise. But until she vanishes their 'Waha! Wahaha! Wahahaha!' does not abate.

Scene 3

Gradually such pranks become rarer, and down dark alleyways between rough wooden shacks, children stand here and there in wait.

If a drunken soldier heaves into view, frond-like hands grab at hardened arms and tug.

'Hello! Ok! Madam nice! Nice! Ok!'

Having had a taste of money, the children have found their own way of exploiting this lamentable reality.

7. (Before a war cemetery of North Korean dead)

Ah, surely they could never close your eyes,
you, souls now resting here in rows?

It was these our hands, that until yesterday
pressed the trigger and took your lives,
that gathered up your broken, rotting bodies, your bones,
then chose a secluded mountainside where the sun is right,
and quietly buried them, even covered the spot with turf,
for truly death is more mysterious
than hatred or love.

Not far from here the road is blocked,
the homeward road your souls, like mine, must take,
and the mere silence of the empty, desert hills
oppresses my breast like a thousand tons;
so while in life we were only united in hate,
now rather the tragic longing
you were not able to allay
dwells within my aspiration.

In the spring sky, nearly close enough to touch,
a cloud indifferently
floats North-ward;
gunfire echoes from afar
and before these tombs of love and hate
all I can do is weep copious tears.

밭
日記
Diary of
the Fields

1

In the fields young shoots appear.
In the fields the leaves unfold.
In the fields the flowers bloom.
In the fields the fruits ripen.

In the fields, what can we do?
All we can do is run errands.

2

Urging on his ox,
the farmer ploughs his field.

The blocked pores of the ground
burst open.

The frozen lungs
expand again.

The spring sky
seems near enough to touch.

Ox and peasant both
look up at it together.

A cloud
drifts North-wards.

Moooo!

The ploughshare bites into the soil,
ripping through
thorns and creepers.

3

Three days married!
Slyly stealing glances at one another,
the young couple treads down the barley field
which, still frozen, creaks beneath their feet.

Filling the deeply engraved ruts with soil,
as if firming up their swelling, restless hearts,
step by step they tread down the soil.

To the East outpouring sunbeams break through,
to the South a haze dances over the hills
like a nylon veil;
on the branches of an old West-leaning tree
yellow and red jackets blossom,
bearing waterpots on their heads;
in the village huddled to the North
the sweet smoke of morning smoothly rises
from chimneys over yellow thatch.

Like motes of dust in a greenhouse,
swarms of gnats dance before my eyes,
the birds flutter, dive and chirp.
A smell drifts across from somewhere,
like chicken manure,
in the morning when the ground first thaws
the whole world exhales beauty.

11 (Van Gogh)

In an ash-coloured sky,
seemingly about to collapse,
inky clouds twist.
The ground, too, looks dark,
as if about to spit ink;
driven like waves before a storm,
flashing pale silver,
the wheat-fields only reinforce
this sense of despair.

'Beneath a sky threatening rain and thunder,
wheat-fields stretch as far as the eye can see;
I have tried to express there
all my sadness or solitude.'

*

Auvers, Sunday July 27, 1890.

There is a sky so clear it seems about to break.
Beneath the dazzling sunlight
the wheat-fields dare not lift their heads,
the air is thick, the silence exhausted,
even the insect sounds seem vast and void.

Like a scarecrow in a fit of madness,
all day long a man wanders raving
through the wheat-fields.
Soon dusk falls.
'I cannot take any more.'
Crack! Crack! Crack!
The sun vomits blood and sets.
The man topples.

*

If you climb the stairway ladder,
there is an attic room
with a window fixed in its sloping ceiling,
a palid lamp with a lolling tongue,
broken-seated chairs,
a cracked mirror where the light flickers,
a vase with crackled glazing,
a floor with gaping planks,
walls of blistered plaster,
a calendar with the wrong date.

On the old iron bed,
covered with a filthy blanket,
after lingering for twenty-eight hours,
at one in the morning of July the twenty-ninth,
the man at last expires.

Against the dead man's breast his brother
finds a single sheet of paper, a will:
'Now I have staked my whole life on painting
and it has destroyed my reason.'

                    *

Hearse-less, the coffin
crosses the wheat-fields.
On the village hill
can be seen the cross of the church
where they refused to lend a hearse.

No end to the wheat-fields.
A little farther on, the cemetery.
In the farthest corner, at the foot of the wall,
two graves lie side by side.

Over that to the left is written
'Ci-gît
Vincent van Gogh
1853–1890'
Over that to the right

'Ci-gît
Théodore van Gogh
1858–1891.'

On the stone,
a hand has laid a bunch of those sunflowers
which in his lifetime set his heart ablaze;
on every side stretch those wheat-fields
he loved to destruction.

27

In the thick forest
where the furnace-sun pours down heat,
hands like great toads
strike fire from a flint
large as a stone on a storage jar
and, parting, set the fire free.

Flames attack the sky.
In a flash the jungle is a sea of flames.

Towering heavenwards, trees
tall as Russians or Yankees,
others with fat trunks
recalling greasy Manchus,
thickly packed bushes
like soldiers of South and North in arms
not understanding the recent madness,
thorn-sharp bushes bristling
with present hates and hostility,
brambles tangled in history's twists,
matted by Destiny's turning wheel,
the forest of all the powers,
down to the roots of every system,
in short, this world's entire dead ground,
with a sound of thunder,
a sound of guns,
is overturned completely and burns.

On the vast deserted mountain heights
where they ruled as undisputed masters,
the tigers, panthers, and other such
flee now with fire at their tails;
bears, badgers and boars,
that had only thought to fill their stomachs,
all fall into blazing trenches and ditches;
snakes, foxes, wolves and wild cats,
all such cunning kind
run hither and thither in search of escape,

their eyes glinting till the end;
owls, bats, and all that steal by night,
the spiders with their information net-works,
the toads, moles, rats, with all such spies and agents,
the bands that eat at every table,
as well as the nests of the birds that sang
and paid no heed to the world's affairs,
yes, even the guiltless little frogs,
all burn.
Stretch dead.
They race around in stifling smoke.
They stumble and roll.
They groan and howl in pain.
Even the blood they shed is consumed,
all crackling, consumed in flames.

A billowing tidal wave of fire!
In this great mountainside blaze
every curse is undone,
every bond is unloosed
from off this land, this people,
Oh, then burn on! Burn on!
Burn a whole month! Burn for three!

Once everything has vanished into smoke and ashes,
once the blood-shedding darkness has gone,
in the peace of the pyre,
in the relief of a mother delivered of child,
behold, a new land!
A plain in which North and South shall be one,
now forcibly divided,
united as flesh closes to heal a wound.

There, as if from Noah's Ark,
see women and men advance
wearing plaited bamboo hats,
with sound of gongs, beating drums,
blowing flutes and clashing cymbals
they advance.
They dig the ground.

They cultivate the fields.
They sow the seed.
In this vast new field,
free at last of the shadowy trace
of the resentful dead, now at peace,
celebrating the world's new dawning,
they shall honour anew none but One,
only the Trinity of autonomy, dilgence, harmony.

28

So far, I have never heard
any voice whatever,
be it from heaven, from earth,
or from men.

Neither have I seen any vision.

Within my breast have blossomed and vanished
billions
upon billions of observations,
but I could not express a single word.

*

Was my soul born, from the very start,
with unseeing eyes?

Day after day, every day
I open wide the eyes of my being
and look up to you, oh Heavens,
but alas encounter no light, only vast emptiness . . .

그리스도 폴의
江

St. Christopher's
River

1

It was merely water.
It was a great mass of water.
That great mass of water
flowed indifferent on.

Flowing on, it always
stayed in the selfsame place.
Staying in the selfsame place,
it was constantly renewed.

Renewed, although the past
continued steadfast there.
The past continued steadfast,
but the future too was there.

Past and future, thus united,
became one single present.
And that single present moment
showed many faces there.

It showed so many faces,
spoke in many voices.
Speaking many voices,
its heart was indifferent to all.

Always to all indifferent, it suffered,
and suffering it was still indifferent.
Indifferent, one day it died
and dying returned to life.

4

The river flows on,
without a filthy heart,
all pure of body,
it flows like time in Eternity.

The river flows on,
without a paltry body,
all pure of heart,
it flows like Eternity in time.

The river flows on,
neither heart nor body,
it flows, an essence of nothingness.

6

The river
continues the past,
is not imprisoned by the past.

The river,
while living today
lives the future too.

The river,
though innumerably collective,
keeps unity and equality.

The river
makes itself an empty mirror
in which all things view themselves.

The river
at all times and in all places
chooses the lowest place.

The river,
unresisting, accepts
every violence, every humiliation,
and never denies itself.

The river
gives freely to all that lives
and looks for nothing in return.

The river
is its own master,
free despite all bonds.

The river,
caught between generation and extinction,
reveals Eternity within impermanence.

The river
every day in its Pantomime
teaches me many things.

8

Beneath the river bed
that our human eyes can see
there flows another river,
deep and wide.

Piercing downwards and sideways,
forming eyes for the lace-like strata,
sparkling like the dawn
in the deepest darkness,
it flows.

And down that silver river
petrified beasts and plants
float like sailing ships,
with at times a human corpse.

And all around those dead things
float, like a thick mist,
those dreams,
and loves,
and tears,
and grudges,
and prayers,
that alive they kept within.

My poetic thoughts are there too,
the things I can neither express nor represent.

10

I have spent today,
that source of mystery, today,
wallowing in the dirt.

Along the sewers of my soul,
so full of stench and running muck,
the spirits of all purity
have foamed and died.

Tomb of Time turned to a muddy slough!
Just a trickle of tears flows from the drain
and drips into the coal-black stream.

Sun and moon too have lost their shine,
and all those things that once bloomed flowers of grace
reciprocate now with a wilting look.

Ah! When will that day come
when my life and all its meaning
will flow into the distant sea
and recover eternal freshness?

13

The river, too,
day by day, depending on the moment,
puts on a different look.

One day,
beaming brightly,
it is full of joy.

Another day,
glowering,
it lies grim.

At times,
emaciated,
it cowers.

At other times,
crimson-faced,
it gets excited.

Other times,
repeatedly
it sighs.

Some days,
sobbing,
it weeps.

Is then the river
so
like my heart?

19

Watching how the river waters
flow around red mountain slopes,
I bring to mind that moment when
a single drop of dew, long seeping
through the crust of earth, sprang out,
a tiny spring high upon a desolate peak.

Watching how the river waters
wind across the verdant fields,
I picture when at last they reach
their destined ocean's waiting vastness
and, flowing into billowing waves,
leap beyond the bounds of time.

Watching how the river waters
flow with perfect ease before me,
I imagine when at last
this river, all transmigration
with repeated evaporations,
and I, the carcass of destiny then thrown off,
will meet again upon this spot as living beings.

20

Laid along the valleys here and there,
having cast off their carcass of flesh and blood,
nothing now but a handful of earth,
here the ancient dead flow by.

Thus the river clasps to its breast
the desires and sorrows of every person
and flows.

So one day, soon, as I flow by,
shall I not encounter
the unthinking gaze of my youngest child
now fishing here,
of his son or grandson, at least?

And then, one day,
all turned to praise,
I shall sit here again myself!

30

The river flows . . .

As the bier carries off the days long past,
and the procession is filled with things yet far away,
so, bearing all the vast emptiness of a long, remote story,

the river flows . . .

bearing the mysterious wonder of the birth
of a tear-like dewdrop that has passed through the earth,
from a secret source like a virgin's fountain

the river flows . . .

murmuring all its mottled yearning,
touching the wounds received in falling
against the rocky sides of bottomless chasms,
slipping through the stony labyrinths of knowledge,

the river flows . . .

colouring with hope and shame,
all the passionate romanticism of the world's vast plains,
the solitude and prayer that arise in marshes,
and, ah, the bitter memories of wandering and chill,

the river flows . . .

now beneath Time's indifferent stare,
bearing in its breast the playfulness of water creatures,
on its back craft of painful labour and of pleasure,
gliding below bridges where good and evil, love and
                                    hatred pass,
hearing whispers of love and songs of parting,
groans of birth, groans of death, the grief of bitter souls,
making symphony with the rhythms of all that lives,

the river flows . . .

in sources and rapids, falls and streams,
all the hosts of being join, mingle, unite,
begetting, dying, flowing into the azure sea
to become the origin of new generation
until history at last, in sinuous fullness, perfectly ends,

the river flows . . .

without any shadow of past or future,
with a constant identity in a world of change,
with a love more solid than any rock,
breathing each present moment in Eternity,

the river flows . . .

with no concern about imminent evaporation,
weeping with desire for non-being,
smiling at the flower of illusion,

the river flows . . .

River! Essence of the unbeing Void!

까마귀

The Crow

1.

Caw caw caw caw.

My friends!
I cannot tell you
how sorry I feel.

The song I long to sing you
is boundless but
my tune is only this
(how sorry I feel):

caw caw caw caw.

2

In the very middle of the highway as the bus speeds
restless onward on a springtime outing, a crow has flown
down, perches there and crows:

Caw caw caw caw!

In days gone by I only had to make my voice heard
in two or three caws from high up in those mountainside
trees for people all to stop and feel troubled about their
present conduct, reflect on their manner of living,
anticipate their own death, even think of Eternity:

Caw caw caw caw!

I really do not know what has got into this present
age; even though I take the trouble to come down and
caw here in the middle of the road, not only is there not
one that stops, but behind their tightly closed car
windows, as they speed on, their faces show surprise
that such a useless flying beast still survives:

Caw caw caw caw!

The way this lot live, exposed to no other songs than
the senseless sound of wandering sparrows being driven
from the roads, or the parrot in a cage at home, or the
warblers' song in a cage at the zoo, frittering away today,
and tomorrow too, in so-called living! It all seems to be
quite ridiculous:

Caw caw caw caw!

In the middle of the highway a crow has flown down
and perches crowing, as if determined to get itself run
over.

3

Erring over mountain slopes
and over the rugged fields,
filling my stomach with carrion and dead bugs,
I am a bird that practises an austere religion
under perpetual vows.

Caw caw caw caw!

Don't get me wrong and think that my voice,
hoarse with a soul's aspirations and tears,
is pouring down imprecations.
My role is only to foretell and announce
the calamities provoked by your injustices,
revealed to the enlightened eyes of my heart.

Caw caw caw caw!

Today as ever, here I am, perched
on the branch of a dead tree on a hill north of Seoul,
observing the daily life that drives you all so frantic,
vested with the foreknowledge and wrath of John the
                                                    Baptist
on the banks of the Jordan, I cry aloud and say:

You vipers, repent!

The Time of the Lord is at hand.
Let anyone who has two tunics
        give one to someone who has none.
Let anyone who has enough to eat
        share it with someone starving.
Let the powerful not oppress the weak
        and use no deception.
The nation's taxes must be moderate,
        levied equitably.
There must be no injustice in collecting them.

Caw caw caw caw!

7

Caw caw
   — You shiver?
Caw caw
   — Yet it's summer!
Caw caw caw
   — A hawk has appeared, they say,
   on the City Hall roof?
Caw caw caw
   — It seems they carry off all the pigeons!
Caw caw caw caw
   — The magpies caught in cages,
   the pigeons carried off!
Caw caw caw caw
   — What a city! Unspeakable!
Caw caw caw caw caw!
   — Won't they catch us too, and crop our wings,
   like the ravens at the Tower of London?
Caw caw!
   — Horror! Horror!

8

Caw
caw
caw
caw
caw
caw
caw
caw
caw
caw
caw
caw
caw
caw
caw
caw
ca . . .
ca . . .
c . . . .
c . . . .
— You are loosing your voice!
— You are getting hoarse!

까옥
까옥
까옥
까옥
까옥
까옥
까옥
까옥
까옥
까옥
까옥
까옥
까옥
까옥
까옥
까옥
깍
깍
칵
칵
—자네 목소린 쉬었군!
—자네 목소린 잠겼군!

International Poetry Series

THE NAKED MACHINE Selected poems of Matthías Johannessen.
Translated from the *Icelandic* by Marshall Brement.
(Forest/Almenna bokáfélagid)
0 948259 44 2 cloth £7.95   0 948259 43 4 paper £5.95   96 pages. Illustrated

ON THE CUTTING EDGE Selected poems of Justo Jorge Padrón.
Translated from the *Spanish* by Louis Bourne.
0 948259 42 6 paper £8.95   176 pages

ROOM WITHOUT WALLS Selected poems of Bo Carpelan.
Translated from the *Swedish* by Anne Born.
0 948259 08 6 paper £7.95   144 pages.   Illustrated

CALL YOURSELF ALIVE? The love poems of Nina Cassian.
Translated from the *Romanian* by Andrea Deletant and
Brenda Walker. Introduction by Fleur Adcock.
0 948259 38 8 paper £6.95.   96 pages.   Illustrated

A VANISHING EMPTINESS Selected poems of Willem M. Roggeman.
Edited by Yann Lovelock. Translated from the *Dutch*.
0 948259 51 5 £7.95   112 pages.   Illustrated

PORTRAIT OF THE ARTIST AS AN ABOMINABLE SNOWMAN
Selected poems of Gabriel Rosenstock translated from the
Irish by Michael Hartnett. New Poems translated by Jason Sommer.
0 948259 56 6 paper £7.95   112 pages   Dual text

LAND AND PEACE Selected poems of Desmond Egan.
Translated *into Irish* by Michael Hartnett, Gabriel Rosenstock,
Douglas Sealey and Tomas MacSiomoin. Dual text.
0 948259 64 7 paper £7.95   112 pages

THE EYE IN THE MIRROR Selected poems of Takis Varvitsiotis.
Translated from the *Greek* by Kimon Friar. (Forest/Paratiritis)
0 948259 59 0 paper £8.95   160 pages

THE WORLD AS IF Selected poems of Uffe Harder.
Translated from the *Danish* by John F. Deane and Uffe Harder.
(Dedalus/Forest)
0 948259 76 0 paper £4.95   80 pages

SPRING TIDE Selected poems of Pia Tafdrup.
Translated from the *Danish* by Anne Born.
0 948259 55 8 paper £7.95   96 pages

SNOW AND SUMMERS Selected poems of Solveig von Schoultz.
Translated from *Finland/Swedish* by Anne Born.
Introduction by Bo Carpelan. Arts Council funded.
0 948259 52 3 paper £7.95   112 pages

FOOTPRINTS OF THE WIND Selected poems of Mateja Matevski.
Translated from the *Macedonian* by Ewald Osers.
Introduction by Robin Skelton. Arts Council funded.
0 948259 41 8 paper £6.95   96 pages. Illustrated

ARIADNE'S THREAD An anthology of contemporary Polish
women poets. Translated from the *Polish* by Susan Bassnett and
Piotr Kuhiwczak. UNESCO collection of representative works.
0 948259 45 0 paper £6.95   96 pages

POETS OF BULGARIA An anthology of contemporary Bulgarian poets.
Edited by William Meredith. Introduction by Alan Brownjohn.
0 948259 39 6 paper £6.95   112 pages

FIRES OF THE SUNFLOWER Selected poems by Ivan Davidkov.
Translated from the *Bulgarian* by Ewald Osers.
0 948259 48 5 paper £6.95   96 pages.   Illustrated

STOLEN FIRE Selected poems by Lyubomir Levchev.
Translated from the *Bulgarian* by Ewald Osers.
Introduction by John Balaban.
UNESCO collection of representative works.
0 948259 04 3 paper £6.95   112 pages.   Illustrated

AN ANTHOLOGY OF CONTEMPORARY ROMANIAN POETRY
Translated by Andrea Deletant and Brenda Walker.
0 9509487 4 8 paper £6.95   112 pages.

GATES OF THE MOMENT Selected poems of Ion Stoica.
Translated from the *Romanian* by Brenda Walker and
Andrea Deletant. Dual text with cassette.
0 9509487 0 5 paper £6.95   126 pages   Cassette £3.50 plus VAT

SILENT VOICES An anthology of contemporary Romanian women
poets. Translated by Andrea Deletant and Brenda Walker.
0 948259 03 5 paper £8.95   172 pages

EXILE ON A PEPPERCORN Selected poems of Mircea Dinescu.
Translated from the *Romanian* by Andrea Deletant and Brenda Walker.
0 948259 00 0 paper £7.95   96 pages.   Illustrated

LET'S TALK ABOUT THE WEATHER Selected poems of Marin Sorescu
Translated from the *Romanian* by Andrea Deletant and Brenda Walker.
0 9509487 8 0 paper £6.95   96 pages

THE ROAD TO FREEDOM Poems and Prose Poems by Geo Milev
Translated from the *Bulgarian* by Ewald Osers.
0 948259 40 X paper £6.95   96 pages   Illustrated

IN CELEBRATION OF MIHAI EMINESCU Selected poems and extracts
translated from the *Romanian* by Brenda Walker and
Horia Florian Popescu. Illustrated by Sabin Balaşa.
0 948259 62 0   Limited edition £20   176 pages

THROUGH THE NEEDLE'S EYE Selected poems of Ion Milos.
Translated from the *Romanian* by Brenda Walker and Ion Milos.
0 948259 61 2 paper £6.95   96 pages.   Illustrated

JOUSTS OF APHRODITE Poems collected from the Greek Anthology Book V
Translated from the *Greek* into modern English by Michael Kelly.
0 948259 05 1 cloth £6.95   0 948259 34 5 paper £4.95   96 pages

POETRY FROM BENGAL An anthology of twentieth century Bengali poets.
Translated from the *Bengali* by Ron Banerjee.
The first book of the UNESCO World Series of Poetry.
0 948259 79 5   paper £8.95   160 pages

FISH RINGS ON WATER Selected poems by Katherine Gallagher,
the *Australian* poet. Introduced by Peter Porter.
0 948259 75 2   paper £6.95   96 pages   Illustrated

PIED POETS An anthology of Romanian Transylvanian and Danube poets
writing in German. Translated from the *German* by Robert Elsie.
Dual text English/German. Arts Council funded
0 948259 77 9   paper £10.95   192 pages

LOVE SONNETS OF THE RENAISSANCE
Translated from the *French, Italian* and *Spanish* and *Portuguese*
by Laurence Kitchin.
0 948259 60 4   paper £6.95   96 pages   Dual text

BEFORE WE WERE STRANGERS Poems by the *American* poet Nadya Aisenberg.
Introduced by Sylvia Kantaris.
0 948259 81 7   paper £6.95   96 pages

CLOSED CIRCUIT by Shadab Vajdi.
Translated from the *Persian* by Lotfali Kohonji and introduced
by Peter Avery.
0 948259 78 7   paper £6.95   96 pages

STEP HUMAN INTO THIS WORLD Poems by Olaf Munzberg.
Translated from the *German* by Mitch Cohen.
0 948259 53 1   paper £6.95   96 pages

ENCHANTING BEASTS An anthology of Finnish women poets.
Translated from the *Finnish* and the *Swedish* by Kirsti Simonsuuri.
0 948259 68 X   paper £8.95   160 pages

International Drama Series

THE THIRST OF THE SALT MOUNTAIN Three plays by Marin Sorescu
(Jonah, The Verger, and the Matrix) Translated from the *Romanian*
by Andrea Deletant and Brenda Walker.
0 9509487 5 6 paper £7.95   124 pages.   Illustrated

VLAD DRACULA THE IMPALER A play by Marin Sorescu
Translated from the *Romanian* by Dennis Deletant.
0 948259 07 8 paper £6.95   112 pages.   Illustrated

International Short Story Series

RUNNING TO THE SHROUDS Six sea stories of Konstantin Stanyukovich.
Translated from the *Russian* by Neil Parsons.
0 948259 06 X paper £6.95   112 pages.

HEARTWORK Stories of Solveig von Schoultz.
Translated from *Finland/Swedish* by Marlaine Delargy and
Joan Tate. Introduction by Bo Carpelan.
0 948259 50 7 paper £7.95   144 pages

THICKHEAD AND OTHER STORIES by Haldun Taner.
Translated from the *Turkish* by Geoffrey Lewis.
UNESCO collection of representative works.
0 948259 58 2 paper £8.95   176 pages

YOUTH WITHOUT YOUTH and other Novellas by Mircea Eliade.
Edited and with an introduction by Matei Calinescu.
Translated from the *Romanian* by MacLinscott Ricketts.
0 948259 74 4 paper £12.95   328 pages

A WOMAN'S HEART Stories by Jordan Yovkov.
Translated from the *Bulgarian* by John Burnip.
0 948259 54 X paper £9.95   208 pages

THE SEER AND OTHER STORIES by Jonas Lie.
Translated from the *Norwegian* by Brian Morton and Richard Trevor.
0 948259 65 5 paper £9.95   208 pages

THE TALISMAN Stories and poems by Ganga Prasad Vimal.
Edited by Wendy Wright. G.L.A. funded.
0 948259 57 4 paper £9.95   208 pages   Dual text English/Hindi.

GH439-B